Abandoned Flowers

Ewan Lawrie

Non-U/KDP

Copyright © 2023 by Ewan Lawrie

All rights reserved.

No part of this publication may be reproduced, distributed, or transmitted in any form or by any means, including photocopying, recording, or other electronic or mechanical methods, without the prior written permission of the publisher, except as permitted by UK. copyright law. For permission requests, contact [include publisher/author contact info].

The story, all names, characters, and incidents portrayed in this production are fictitious. No identification with actual persons (living or deceased), places, buildings, and products is intended or should be inferred.

Book Cover by Author

1st edition 2023

Contents

1. Fading Flowers — 1
2. Exotic Blooms — 19
3. Flowers At The Bedside — 41
4. Roadside Flowers — 55
5. Flowers In Wreaths — 71
6. "Blooming Lilacs" — 91

Acknowledgements — 119

Also By Ewan Lawrie — 121

Fading Flowers

- Hearts and Flowers
- Holding On
- The Road Goes
- We Look Back
- Looking For Trouble
- Tempus Fugit
- And...
- Self-Portrait
- Whistles
- Benches
- I Believe

Hearts And Flowers

If you've seen the lion's tooth

piercing the pavement flags,

know that its roots

are turning concrete

to sand.

You'll know the city's hearts

decorate shadow streets

- with tags for names

in lurid spray paint

on bricks.

There is urban romance

gilding the hollow shops:

the sun makes odd

rainbows in puddles

of oil.

I hear the mongrels sing,

howling at street-lamp moons

because their light

is always full

but blurred.

A symphony plays on

junkyard instruments

metal on metal

and siren screams

of girls.

Between the luxury

and the tourist traps

are poverty's weeds,

still growing here,

and now.

Holding On

You're holding tight
to the slippery rope.
Are you climbing,
up to the sunlight
above the clouds
where the uplands
used to be?
Are you descending,
down to Sheol,
via Purgatory,
across the Styx
to Albion?
Are you paralysed
with icy fear
or indecision
and the demon
of doubt?
You're holding tight:
you could let go,
you might rise;
a balloon
on the
wind.
Or

ABANDONED FLOWERS

you

might

fall

into

d

e

s

p

a

i

r.

The Road Goes

I am glad,

pleased to be on the downward slope,

hope lies on the other side of the hill;

the upward, where the eyes on the prize

care not for roadside flowers,

miss the tares and muddy ditches,

in the joy of having a goal.

Though hope is

foolish on the steepening decline,

mine flickers yet, seeing beauty

in the rabbits still in fields,

despite the chemical death

between corn and barley,

in fields regrown at last.

At road's end

the dandelion countdown reads nil,

still I wonder what comes next,

if anything, or will I too

return to earth and dust

and wait for wildflowers to poke

through my bleached bones .

We Look Back

We look back at a rose-coloured past,

forget the daily drudgery and drink

in the sweetly happy elixir of our youth.

We look back at a slim and smiling face

before our dissolution, and say

"no regrets" to the blurred facsimile in our mirror.

We look back at a strange-routed past,

ignore the simple signs on our way

to the lambent sun-blissed exile of our now.

We look back at our rare and random choice

at every binary fork and wish

"noli me tangere" had been the watchword in our journal.

We look back at a long- admired self,

believe the written words in our script

on the yellowed, mildewed paper in a drawer.

We look back at our sweet and sour love

for all the golden girls we kissed

"I love you" while they whispered no-one's name.

Looking For Trouble

Like Lorca's, my friends looked for me

in bars, brothels and bridewells.

They found me though, from time to time.

But often I'd be full-crocked

in Joe's, Joey's and Joseph's

in conversation man-to-man

like bosom barflies singing drunk

with Fritz, Franco or Fintan

in lifeboats sailing from bar-to-bar.

Like Judas I would tell my friends

to vroom, vavoom or vanish

in taxis back to real-to-real life,

But truly, I loved the fact they came

to joints, jukes and jails

and found me in my home from home.

Tempus Fugit

We are middling old,

muddling words, forgetting names,

becoming gnomes, shrinking fast,

fearing lost memories.

We, the quondam young,

knew yin and yang, hated parents

ignored their guidance, protested loud,

sometimes laid each other.

You will also age,

ever-so fast; good looks lost,

shaking your fist, and feeling bitter,

you will matter no more

And...

Though the minutes seem like hours,

the days are swiftly gone,

like wind-blown calendar leaves

in a black-and-white movie.

My hourglass is an egg-timer,

the sand is sharp as ever was.

Even though I'm not asking,

the bell is telling me.

The waves are rushing in

to sweep my footprints away.

Self-Portrait

The portrait in my mirror,
shows in pentimenti
someone I used to be:
life has painted experience over
youth's cartoon, whose bold lines
are all but hidden by impasto.
These colours' oils are fat-based.

The light-source is not kind,
creating chiaroscuro in shadows
under still bright eyes.
"By fifty we have the face
we deserve", as Eric said.
Ten years later it is clear
how deserving we have been.

I will not reform the image
in the silvered glass, nor make needled
interventions to conjure a pop-art
caricature of someone I never was.
This face is mine, I have made it.

Whistles

Two notes: never heard a wolf whistle.

Any more than I heard a pierced-beak blackbird

trill a five note arpeggio.

Train whistle

"All aboard!

Morningtown

next stop."

Playground whistle,

playtime over

school is in.

One long note -never heard the factory whistle;

never worked on a production line,

never worked to rule.

There are no bells

or whistles, on us

- we underlings

are the basic model.

ABANDONED FLOWERS

There's a whistle

we all expect

- sooner or later -

and it signals

the end of the game.

Maybe there's an echo

of the time

you whistled down the wind.

Benches

I sat on the bench on the High Row,

like an old man, or a tramp:

17 years old, wearing a charity-shop

greatcoat and a prog-rocker's haircut,

listening to the Clash and the Pistols

in my head: another year to wait

before the Sony Walkman Cassette Player

let us take our music everywhere.

That boy is missing,

long disappeared,

though his hairstyle is

back in the stylish greys

of an "anteek" filter.

The music is played

in the flat keys

of hexadecimal code.

I sit on other benches,

an old man, like a tramp,

60 years old wearing a three-quarter

Kray coat and a Bahrain-souk keffiyah

worn like a scarf against the cold

unfelt by that boy from so long ago,

before the sun touched northern skin,

when adventure took him everywhere.

I Believe

I believe

in leaving coins

on the table or the bar,

just in case I pass that way again,

the price of a smile

beside an empty glass.

I believe

a woman can

wear hoops, big enough

to wear as anklets,

in her ears, if her

hair is long at sixty.

I believe

I'll die happy

on the other side of

the sky with El Dorado's gold

piled near a rainbow's

end and a blue bird.

I believe

in true lovers,

outside of celluloid and

wood-pulped pages with

faded ink printed in tear-smeared

lines of deadly prose.

I believe

a shaman can

call ghosts by surnames

out of a cuff-link or a nail cutting

stolen from a corpse

in a lined coffin.

I believe

we've talked quite

enough

about me.

Exotic Blooms

- Cold Paradise
- Paseo Maritimo
- Mad Dogs And Englishmen
- February Morning
- Dusting
- Photograph
- Beach
- Listen
- Weather Report
- Autumn Comes
- Málaga
- Sahara Sand
- Bajondillo
- Café-Bar Ísabel
- Moonlight Over Seville
- Pavement Diamonds

Cold Paradise

As bitter as a Seville orange,

the wind bites and blows

the plastic bags and cans

around the rusting wheelie bin.

A skeletal pye-dog cocks a leg

absently rusting already tired metal;

an alien number plate rushes past

- children late for class-

by a year and ten minutes.

A lone and grubby child's sock

fruits a bedraggled bush;

the sun cannot return

soon enough to save it.

Paseo Maritimo

The weathered wooden boards
snake between sharp sand
and rocks protesting their treatment
by the cold Atlantic waves.
There's a sea fret,
but the Spanish words for
fog and mist and ghosts
are mumbled by the brisk walkers
along the Paseo Maritimo.
Shapes are visible - or imagined -
in the salt-damp gloom.
Armada vessels bound for defeat,
Marie Celestes, Flying Dutchmen,
or countless nameless wrecks
tracing doomed routes
through the Galician fog.
Azure blue cracks the grey,
it's shocking that no sound
accompanies this surprising thing
and that in twenty short minutes
the Atlantic looks
like the Caribbean.

Mad Dogs And Englishmen

Behind country restaurants,

in front of town bars,

on sun-cracked flags,

café-cultured customers

drink too fast, too much.

The heat, the sun

give a man a thirst

to let others see him

at his red-skinned worst.

Local people - with local ways -

are asleep behind blinds

shaded by shutters;

dream long, dream sweet:

the cool, the dark,

give a man a rest

and let others see him

at his sleep-saved best.

ABANDONED FLOWERS

  Under cars and canopies,

in ditches dry of water,

behind skips and bins -

pye-dogs, curs and strays.

The shade, the peace:

give a dog a bone

and let others see him

at the last alone.

Along the high road,

across baked, cracked fields,

crazed Cereberus

runs amok in muck:

the flies, the pain,

"mad dogs and Englishmen":

one and the same,

out in the midday sun.

February Morning

It's the time for wood-smoke;

olive trees are being stripped,

straw hats bend over the piled

and twisted wooden limbs,

the snapcrackle flames riskily close.

The bitter smell obscures

and shortens further

the brief glory

of the almond blossom.

Dusting

Snowy talc has fallen on the many-toothed peaks

- sierra is Spanish for saw - after all.

Bitter days with the coldest blue sky

the colour of Estonian eyes:

There are plenty of those on the Costa -

if you know where to look.

Just one day of sunshine swipes

the powder from the mountain tops,

clouds clear and *this* blue is warmer

than a pole-dancer's eyes.

Photograph

A trattoria, all gingham cloths

and chianti bottle lamps,

looks onto a square

in the wrong Latin country.

Gianni knows very well

the feminine is unchanged here,

but 'il' becomes 'el' outside

the doors of 'Il Griglio Parlante'.

On the restaurant walls

are monochrome memories

from the days of bombazined matrons

to those of mini-skirted smoking girls.

Over a table in a quiet corner

is Gianni's favourite photograph.

In a still cobbled Rome, boys on Vespas

and slit-eyed old men stare after elegance.

ABANDONED FLOWERS

The woman, wasp-waisted, has her back

to the unknown photographer.

Her arms are bare, though her white-gloved hands

carry a clutch-bag that matches her shoes.

The skirt of her Schiparelli dress is A-line,

Gianni tells me over many Grappas

that the woman in the photo is La Loren.

All the men's faces tell me this is true.

Beach

Fierce:

rocks, black and smoothed.

A sculptor-God made this Atlantic beach.

Random, unexpected shapes in granite.

Some millennial visitor has liveried one

in ocean-liner red and black; Titanic whited

on the prow of this shiprock.

Shapes:

here a dolphin,

there an abstract of solid drama.

Their forms burst out of parched grass,

cold eruptions from the earth's guts.

There, in front, the sharp, coarse sand

like shattered pieces of the glass it could become.

Past:

a smugglers' beach?

Or the hopeful despatch of a bottled message

from sailors ill-met by those self-same rocks

guarding the interior from the sea

and all who fail on her savage spume?

Or nothing? Not even a fisherman's cove?

Listen

Listen for the rustle of the curling, falling leaves,

listen for birds resting, far from nesting, in the eves.

Summer slips out,

sunshine-boy hat doffed,

sky overdressed in louring clouds

full of sticky, slicky rain.

Listen for the movement of the gasping, thirsty ground,

listen for sheep bleating, something fleeting in the sound.

Autumn strolls in,

grey overcoat buttoned,

town underwhelmed by shorter days

spent in dusty, fusty bars.

Listen for the message of the passing, fading year

listen for me sighing, not yet dying - I'm still here.

Weather Report

There are winds,

howling like dogs; though the beige sun is out.

Roof tiles fall,

spatchcocked in the streets between the potholes.

Rain's coming

louring clouds threaten the craven sunlight.

The trees bend;

they'll break today; branches stolen by gale force

will sail down

flooded arroyos to inappropriate streets.

Autumn Comes

Autumn comes in fiery colours,

the leaves turn auburn, ochre and saffron:

the sun sets low and dyes the sky vermillion.

Autumn comes; in fiery colours

the heat is dulling, cooling and fading:

the goats shiver and bleat on the hillsides

Autumn comes. In fiery colours,

the leaves are drying, crackling and falling:

we harvest the corn, 'til winter begins the dying.

Málaga

Look up,

away from teeming

streets of Malagueños.

Look up,

leave the swelter

seething, boiling in streets

hard baked by July:

hot-foot-tap-dance

in Larios.

Look up,

toward apartments,

laundry flags waving proud.

Look up,

above tapas bars,

cyber-caffs, bakeries

and language schools

selling English

by the kilo.

ABANDONED FLOWERS

Look up,

leave the driver

to the jamming traffic.

Look up,

at the aerial

forest glinting metal-

heliographed babble

in return for

sound and vision.

Look up,

further still to

a sky of aching blue.

Look up,

find one errant

cloud among the contrails,

and enjoy the

impossible

raindrops' falling.

Sahara Sand

Wind-borne sand hangs in the air.

These dry clouds hide the local town,

the Sierra and the sky's cerulean blue.

Rain or a wind-change will rid us

of the dust, carried here – perhaps - with

gunpowder from Fez

or kíf ash from Marrakesh.

If clouds burst and rain red mud,

gutters and streets will run dirty

with litter and the town's promiscuous waste.

It has no name here but dust,

though they do call the adherent wind

Calima, Africus, or - in jest -

the stern-wind of Phoenicians.

Bajondillo

The gypsy quarter squats above the fairground,

waiting all year for the Feria and the arrival

of second and third cousins or sworn enemies.

The Gitanos ready cocks for battle, play pachisi

no Hindu would recognise amid finos tossed back

with gusto and shouts of "¡anda!" or "¡venga!".

They warm their hands over fires in wheelbarrows

used as portable braziers filled with firewood

of most uncertain provenance.

The gamey smell of roasted rabbit permeates

both sides of the street though washing still

hangs on lines and rotary devices after dark.

In scruffy grass between two tumbledown houses

pure breed Spanish horses munch, meditate and move

no more than occasionally, despite the noise.

The Policia Local's car patrols, crawling through a gauntlet

of catcalls, waiting for children crossing the road

as slowly as only toddlers under granny's eye will.

The brave and the foolish take the rat-run

after dark, rushing home, saving kilometres

but wasting heartbeats under glassy, heated stares.

Café-Bar Ísabel

They meet every day,

The Dirty Half-Dozen.

It's not so easy –

nor worthwhile – alone, after 70.

Besides, they sit outside,

talking, smoking, joking

and remembering.

Sons of Nationalists and Communists,

citizens of the New Spain, they sit

reading their past in coffee grounds

and one Ponché, for the road.

A van shudders past, its engine survives

the removal of the key for a few moments.

Pepe waves at people his father's age

and sees his future on the terrace

of a small town café.

Moonlight Over Seville

Under the smiling half moon,

before it waxes gibbous,

shadows hint at silver and

secrets can be kept.

The cobbles glint in moonlight

after the twilit rain;

lovers take the side-streets

and dimmer cul-de sacs.

Along the Alameda,

under the drooping trees,

boys call after chicas but

mothers make reply.

Outside the grave cathedral,

where the phaetons wait:

tourists take their chances

and spring the usual traps.

On Calle Divina Pastora

there's not a sign of sheep:

just the sound of a somnolent city

under the lustrous moon.

Pavement Diamonds

After the slicking rain,

when the sun comes out

and Iris flies overhead,

out of reach except

from the corner of an eye,

as the last steam rises

from an erstwhile puddle,

you glimpse a diamond-sparkle

on pavement flags.

Hopscotching

remaining pools,

you wish for chalk

and pebbles

in your pocket.

Your smile isn't for

the café-terrace waitress,

but you get one

in return.

ABANDONED FLOWERS

Flowers At The Bedside

- Consulting The Runes
- Waiting Room
- Ghosts
- Cooking
- Through the Crooked Glass
- Another Day
- Wishes

Consulting The Runes

We are hunched, afraid,

waiting for the shaman

with his celluloid pictures

that show the insides,

but nobody's soul.

He comes with confidence

armed with a stethoscope

and invulnerability.

Armoured by ... what?

Indifference?

One of us is sick,

but I am nauseous.

It is not I who

has the beast inside,

growing and malignant

All the facts and figures

probability and percentages

fly in one ear and straight

to my bowels, loosened

by fear and rage.

ABANDONED FLOWERS

I make a joke,

nobody laughs,

not even the shaman

or his blue-clad handmaiden.

Waiting Room

Some faces look familiar,

haunted, haggard faces:

you've seen some of them in the mirror.

Strangely, it's hard to tell.

Who has the mark upon them

and who is devastated by proxy?

The young woman, tense and brittle;

her pensioner father not reading a paper;

her mother nervously picking at a resewn hem?

The lanyard-ed passes mark out

the healthy; the healers, immune

to all the misery and apprehension,

at least that's how it looks.

And the chorus walks into the audience,

singing the rich variety of names,

underlining the diversity inherent in disease.

We look up at each herald,

calling out the summons to whatever

is waiting for us in the confessional consulting room.

And we wait,

we wait for news,

good and bad and barely comprehensible.

The young woman comes out,

both her parents crying, each holding the other up,

she shakes her head, it's hard to know what to say

when your prognosis is not good.

Ghosts

We felt we were haunting ourselves.

Shadows of who we'd been.

I stopped looking in the mirror,

who was this hopeless, helpless person,

who could not make it right?

I plastered on a smile:

it slipped,

melting in the heat

of an argument or two.

The kryptonite

was killing the disease

and Superwoman too,

I felt like Mister Mxyzptlk.

accidents didn't happen
in our perfect world:
the hardest parts
fade away and radiate

ABANDONED FLOWERS

80's songs helped,

expecially Debbie

and her band's.

Who knew about

the heart of glass

those poisoned draughts

might give you?

I found spirits

in the songs

and they chased away

the ghosts.

Cooking

You never see it on TV.

None of the judges have it,

so it all tastes great -

or bad -

not metallic.

No one's doing

The Hairless Bikers' Best of British

(and you'll need it),

The Great British Chemo Diet,

or Cancerchef.

No one would win.

Nothing beats the first food

they've enjoyed for a year;

not Ramsay, not Martin,

not Oliver, not Nigella, and no,

not even fucking Blumenthal.

Another Day

Something comes up,

a number that isn't quite right.

Another day, another test.

It's a trial, in more than one sense.

We are lucky:

good or bad, the news is early

and plans can be changed or remade.

The test is the trial and the trial is the test.

What of others?

Those not on trial,

un-summoned by Dr.Uids

for quarterly readings of the runes?

Through the Crooked Glass (or Alec in Wond-Elland)

It's more than a year

since Alice and I tumbled

headlong down the rabbit hole.

The Red Queen encouraged

the executioner's act,

but no *head* was cut off.

Drink Me was not an option,

as the elixir fed

through Alice's veins,

as it still does,

every three weeks

as regular as the clockwork

in the Mad Hatter's watch.

Yes, I am in Wond-Elland,

where everyone speaks

like Keith Lemon

- though he is made-up too.

Lump hammers appear

in roadside conversations,

and praise of cheeseboards

will ring out over pub hubbub.

ABANDONED FLOWERS

On the bus are Poundshop

Michelle Keegans, babies

and upward-punching

husbands in tow.

But I revel

in the babbled babel

of the full five-oh-three.

Polish, Portuguese

and the patois

of 2nd generation

immigrants in leisure-wear

with Strictly-sequinned stripes

down the trouser leg.

It has been difficult,

this adventure

through the crooked glass,

we have fought off

The Red Queen,

but still Alice takes

the elixir, against

the day of a return.

When March comes,

we'll welcome the hare,

mad or no, it can be no worse

than following the rabbit.

It is fine.

I am fine.

My middle name

is Alexander

and though of late

I haven't been so very great,

things are getting better.

Wishes

If it's the last thing we ever do,

We'll be happy,

If there's not a single thing left to do,

We'll be finished.

If there's a place left to visit,

We'll be travelling.

If there's something left to wish for

We'll be hoping.

EWAN LAWRIE

Roadside Flowers

- Bonesack
- The Low Men
- A Coin For Belisarius
- Old Soldiers
- Ghost Furniture
- Corner Poet

Bonesack

Two-layer dressed

in a four-layer wind,

Maggie haunts the doorways.

No-one hangs coffee here,

'Hanging's too good for 'em'.

Whoever 'them' might be.

There, but for the grace

of money and shelter,

go you and I.

Under the sightline,

never a headline

in the newspapers

down the trouser legs

and ripped puffa sleeves.

Have you noticed?

The last family-run

electrics shop in

Anytown

has no TV

in the window.

Maggie has.

Part-time police

move her on,

politeness itself,

minus eye-contact.

It's the doorway

at B & M tonight.

'Maggie carries the bones

of her parents in her sack,'

the children whisper as

they pass not one, but

two, bone-sacks.

The Low Men

we are the low men

low in rank and status

we are the low men

we live with our low spice

a spousal plural

as strong as any drug

for we are of an age

with our grandparents

at their funeral

though we have drunk more

than they could afford

for their lifetime

We   Are

                                                                          The

                                        Low

Men

inside us is shame

and venomous pride

that will poison us

before we tug the forelock

and bend the knee

to the high-heidyins

who look so far down

upon us that we are   *barely seen*

ABANDONED FLOWERS

Wearethelowmen

we whisper it in public

smashthewords

to get her

                         the

                         one

                         we

                         once

                         loved

we are not

shallow

our depths

are not still

                    we are not

                        hollow

                nor are we stuffed

                this land is wasted

                  blasted curséd

                        and...

we are not

streetcorner

scarecrows

to frit the unwary

EWAN LAWRIE

we are the low men

but we are men

A Coin For Belisarius

He's the broken figure on that pub sign,

where Jack the Hat saw another's death

under Belisarius's begging bowl:

the two twins interred themselves now;

characters undreamed of by war poets

turned novelists, in exile.

Our Belisarius huddles in London doorways,

far from the easternized East End;

no helmet for his call to alms,

simply an incongruous schoolboy cap

filled with smaller, duller coins.

He's whistling meanwhile.

The former soldier doesn't see

the taxi-cabs and transit vans,

or pedestrian fraternity.

Lurching tanks and armoured cars

and more bloody infantry

pass his vacant smile.

EWAN LAWRIE

The Last of the Romans is far from

Germania and has long since left

behind the modern Ostrogoth

of flowing beard and Mahdi glint,

save in the battlefield of his dreams

and waking nightmares vile.

Old Soldiers

Nostalgia

There *were* good things,

simple things, often.

A pal giving you his last fag.

The adjutant passing a flask:

brandy from a bar

far from the trenches.

A kiss blown through a window,

at the batallion marching past:

every Tommy thought it meant

for him.

Soldier's Heart

From Gilgamesh to Glasgow Jock on the pavement,

a soldier's heart is broken by dreams

of death and noise and fear.

The blind soldier at Marathon could not see,

because he would not see,

the death of another friend.

Shell Shock

It was a noise

a noise like no other:

sometimes a warning scream,

others simply the thunder

of an angry God.

Oh! The time it rained

limbs and blood.

No wonder some

beat a retreat

to silence

or catatonia.

PTSD

It sounds so new,

so scientific,

measurable

and specific:

simpler for all,

except for those

who have it.

Ghost Furniture

Hautboys, occasional tables,
chipped chippendale
imitations - out of place,
out of doors, on the pavement,
outside Harrison's Butchers -
as was - before Ocado
slaughtered them.

Torn vinyl, seventies sofas
two-and-a-half-piece suites,
not so much sprung
as ham-strung -
not even an old ha'penny
hidden down the back,
since it's post-decimal
upholstery.

There's always a cooker,
electric, grill-over-oven,
under the hob,
traces of grease around the
half-turned knobs
all set at different
temperatures.

EWAN LAWRIE

Radiograms, hat stands

faux elephant's foot

with no umbrellas

and no purpose -

no more than the

nests of tables

empty of their

ashtray nestlings.

Joe's in the doorway

thumbs in his waistcoat

like that man on the telly;

it'll be time to move

it all inside soon.

On the wireless

inside someone sings

about a brilliant mind.

Corner Poet

"We are meant to be paired,

the only even prime is two,

only matching halves

can make a whole."

                The corner poet

                is half-preacher,

                half-madman

                in a lady's coat

                and wellingtons.

                                If the weather turns,

                                he takes shelter

                                in the Savile:

                                he's barred from other bars,

              between closed banks

                the charity shops

                and beauticians,

            where the middle class

                slum it weekly

-if it's market day
and artisan cheese
can be had for pounds
per forty grams.

                                                  Sometimes he shouts
                                                  in the market square,
                                                  from the bandstand
                                                  at the passing traffic
                                                  heading elsewhere.

                       I wonder where
                       he lost the half
                       that used to
                       make him whole?

ABANDONED FLOWERS

Flowers In Wreaths

- The Man On The Other End Of The Phone
- My Father's Diaries
- Here Are Things
- A Visitable Past
- The Woman On The Other Side Of The Screen
- Hereafter
- For As Long As
- Ask Not
- Gentlemen And Players

EWAN LAWRIE

The Man On The Other End Of The Phone

He says hello and my name,

as if trying either out

for the very first time.

My accent becomes his,

maybe there was a school-friend

or drinking pal whose name I bear.

So I reflect his tones and argot

from north of the border

or West of the Pecos

from when he used to read

to me from Zane Grey,

when death came from a six-gun

or a feathered shaft.

Not this slow, creeping un-death...

ABANDONED FLOWERS

I make him laugh, God knows how,

or why I laugh with him.

We talk about Rangers

and I picture Souness,

while he can *see* Slim Jim

or maybe Willie Waddell.

But he loses the thread, laughs again:

so I talk about Clyde puffers

and what the Air Force

was like long before

I followed him in,

like all good sons attempting

just a tiny connection…

before *se cortara la llamada.**

*the call is ended

Memory Games

The result reader's sing-song incantation lists

seaside resorts and grimy, defeated factory towns.

I hear that Bournemouth are going up

and Wigan are - probably - going down.

I think back to days

when the last thing mentioned

at 5 pm on Saturdays

was the pools forecast,

which my dad claimed

was a game of skill

not chance.

Later the b-list chancer is smiling sincerely;

laughing as he reads the balls' numbers out

I hear that Florida or the Costa Del Sol

are places that players can dream about.

ABANDONED FLOWERS

I think of my dad

and the Rangers Pools,

tombola and raffles

in Sergeants' Messes

over distant horizons,

where his memory

lives now.

Memory's lottery has no winning ticket,

the X-es on the coupon are crossings out.

I hear the sound of distant drums,

my father - the past's unceasing, deafening shout.

EWAN LAWRIE

My Father's Diaries

Beside the desk

on an over-booked shelf

are some of my father's diaries.

Three slim, faux-leather,

pocket versions of two

golfing years and a

Darlington Diary.

Two are safe to read

with the aid of

a jeweller's loupe,

though I still feel

like a fence

inspecting

stolen goods.

One is not.

We played golf

he and I,

one June 21st:

we got lost

on the way:

my dad had

driven there

for a quarter

century.

20 years ago sees

still smaller writing:

I cannot read it all,

just odd words

like 'forgot'

and 'remembered'.

The entries end

on December 21st

- after patchy

months of

hieroglyphs.

I will keep

them safe,

still.

EWAN LAWRIE

Here Are Things

A photograph,

he looks like me,

though in monochrome;

an image produced

from celluloid

now cracked

in a paper-sleeve.

A yellow-metal watch,

he used to wear,

on special occasions,

long past the time

he could

tell it,

or the day of the week.

A military tie,

now I have two,

though mine is newer

and I didn't buy it;

not worn in years,

like his,

kept against the day.

ABANDONED FLOWERS

Here are things:

they were his,

they are mine,

they aren't him.

The Visitable Past

I inoculate myself with photographs

of once-vibrant parents

younger than I am now.

These almost banish the memory

of my father's husk;

immobile and staring

in an amyloid prison

papered with photographs

of the strangers called family.

For it is my mother's turn

to feel the slipping

of words and time.

We conduct shouted phone calls weekly;

weakly understood, her deafness

thickens the inexorable fog.

Still, a clandestine visit

is occasionally made

but compassion is no visa

to cross plague-shut borders

where once none existed.

ABANDONED FLOWERS

I must go,

while there is yet

a visitable past,

before she moves

to another country

I cannot reach by phone.

The Woman On The Other Side Of The Screen

There are no names here,

in the digital make-believe of Skype,

where I can see a woman,

who used to be my mother.

My sainted sister says my name,

finger pointed into the tablet screen

to where my face can be seen

but not recognised.

So I shout, the data freeze

makes my name unintelligible

- but it doesn't matter, really -

it falls on deaf ears.

I make faces, childish I know,

but it makes her laugh:

she'll make faces too,

both are better than tears.

A ramble may begin,

my sister will follow

- better than I -

into the darkness of speech.

ABANDONED FLOWERS

I pick out two phrases,
"When" and "Going home"
but they are surrounded
by disjunctive words.

These rambles career
from decade to decade
colliding with names I don't know
and slang words from a past long gone.

After twenty minutes of gestures
I wave my goodbyes
and my mother blows me kisses,
as though I were a mis-remembered beau.

The mouse clicks and the screen goes dark:
how cruel it is, that my mother wanders
in the same curséd forest
where my father, too, was lost.

Hereafter

Some call it "The Hereafter",

as if it were somewhere close,

and not yonder, beyond our ken,

certainly beyond belief,

at least mine.

But there is comfort there,

for those still here -

and those on the threshold,

listening for the piper

at the gates of dawn.

For she, too, heard drums,

different beats,

in syncopated time,

jumping from now to then

stumbling over the previous minutes.

And these drums,

these cruel tympani,

played in her deaf ears

as they had in my father's,

until he too heard pipes.

ABANDONED FLOWERS

So we console ourselves,

with their strong beliefs,

held a lifetime

and know that *they* knew

they'd be together again,

on the other side of the sky,

at the back of the north wind.

For As Long As

Whether our passing is marked

as cind'rous remains

in pottery or pewter vessels,

victims of a well-urned fate;

or as a box-meal for

a generation of worms;

or as near-smoothed,

once sharp-carved letters

on a leaning headstone

in an agnostic cemetery;

or even by a lit candle

near the entrance to a church,

for as long as someone

remembers us, we still live.

Ask Not

In the park,

up on the high Edge,

overlooking the valley and its silent mills,

the leaves fall;

orange, ochre, sienna

and even a hot vermillion.

Around the figure

on its pedestal,

branches have kept their counsel:

 the old flagstones

named after the county

are bare of discarded foliage.

The list of names

has Smiths, Browns, Wilsons

and a dozen multi-syllabic, white-rose signifiers.

A woman cries,

both sides bemedalled

and none speak to ask for whom the tears fall.

At eleven,

the church bells ring

tolling for the long dead, from a mile away.

Gentlemen And Players

We are long in tooth,

we meet at funerals, wakes and memorials,

some's hair is long,

some have none.

Backs are stooped,

faces lined:

some of us limp.

Knees, hips, ankles:

old bones complain,

but we do not.

We have worn the shite-hawk:

we have served in deserts,

inhospitable places, some more than others,

but none said no.

Passes weren't dropped,

tackles were made.

No true sport is war

by other means,

no armistice was celebrated

by so very much drink.

We are thirty years older:

we meet at beer calls, games and reunions,

all of us remain,

including those who've gone.

"Blooming Lilacs"

"Now that lilacs are in bloom..." Prufrock and Other Observations, T S Eliot

- Tom's Swiss Cure
- Evening Walk In A Seaside Town
- Be Prepared
- There, At The World's End
- Urban(e) Voodoo
- Shoah And Tell
- Friday At 8
- These Are The End Times
- Faces
- The Green Man
- Here Is Movement

Tom's Swiss Cure

Let *us* take Tom's Swiss Cure:

look at the mountains beyond the lake

as we come up for the last time, for air

                                             - we dare

to strive, to stay alive, despite

a tragedian's death-wish

to drown ourselves in the Styx;

to cross Charon's palm

with a counterfeit obol,

at last

                               - fast-tied against the mast

like Odysseus listening to the siren song

of mermaids or manatees

[I have heard them and

they have driven me mad].

                           Bad, as I am inclined to be,

I will not swim in an inland sea

rather fly above it seeking caves

of Al a Dín, Saladín and Bin Ladén

- the evil ones – who find us equally so.

ABANDONED FLOWERS

                        Was there love?
What girl can be a flower? What flower can be a girl?
A water lily? The frog prince sits on a lily pad,
glad of any number of kisses from any princess
or pauper girl selling matches in the gutter.

                        And all the words,
every one impersonal: see! The very word
contains a clue, every poet is an imp
and the poet is the poem, after all.

                        Thus we are cured,
of a sudden, as the clock strikes thirteen
and we shall scatter our verses into the wind.

Shan't we?

                    Shan't we?

                                                Shan't we?

Evening Walk In A Seaside Town

Prufrock's Companion

Strewn behind us, I can see the skins of former lives,

trousers pin-striped, soldier's parade-serge

and even battle dress, though I fought

at far remove from blood and bullets.

Let us go then, you and I

to where the future surely lies

at the foot of the hill;

where the tombstone milestone

reads our three score and ten,

or the hundred-and-one

of some unlucky men.

And if we'd asked,

looked beyond the gypsy's curtain,

passed the silver to gnarling knuckles,

for crystal-scrying most uncertain?

Imagine, the crone's tent or pier-end

poster-paint clap-board booth.

"Fortunes told, enquire within"

We'd feel the goosebumps on our skin.

Madame Blandini

A corvid figure, crouched in her chair,
her pitch-black scarf covers her hair,
she chooses her words with consummate care,
with the aid of a pin and *La Dictionnaire.*

No matter her speaking makes no sense,
she writhes with passion, her words intense.
For nothing "begins"- it must commence,
for nonsense predictions, small recompense.

"Woe betide the poetry man,
who writes what he knows,
who writes what he can."

The palm opens, the coin is gone
"I'll need another to carry on."

And she tells it all,
such a bitter truth,
looks back at the mis-steps,
the folly of youth.
Of foolish, unre*quir*ed love,
still less than unrequited.

We give her unkind, parting words:

"Light a candle, cast a spell,

speak in runes, you might as well".

Twilight Time

But we did not go,

we passed the pier by

and made our promenade

along the sea-front

as the sun drowned

in flat grey water

off Margate or Brighton Beach.

And *if* we'd gone,

down the dingy dungeon stairs

into that other world,

of secret, sequinned, he who dares?

Stearns in Clubland

Watchful eyes, used to the dark,

welcome us together,

how can they not?

You and I: we are as inseparable

as Castor and Pollux,

Hermes and Aphrodite,

ego and id.

There are hands linked

across single-candled tables,

they disconnect briefly,

then reconnect as we pass by

and "sit-ye-down"

anent a whispered

request or permission

at an ill-lit table

of our own.

My one drink is cheap

for freedom comes gratis

with it, though there are

no hands across this table.

Coda

And in that bar a mermaid sang

to other mermaids and

-for once, just this once-

for you and me.

Be Prepared

Pay attention, ladies and gentlemen,

this is not the naming of parts,

nor any practical use.

This is duck and cover

for the post-digital age

the dystopic result

of the childish rage

of tyrants.

                                          Post Apocalypse Survivors Kit Mk. 1

                                              There will not be a second version,

                                  when the atomic cloud blacks out the sun.

                                    In the flame-retardant, lead-lined case

                                                each useless item has its place.

The gas mask

is not guaranteed against

every microbe borne

on the nuclear winter's wind.   This blister pack

                                contains placebos only:

                      take them, and chance to luck:

                         they could have been viagra

                             or anti-histamines.

ABANDONED FLOWERS

                                              Your compass will guide

                                       you north, east, west or south,

                                  and all degrees of separation

                                                        in between,

                                                but not to safety.

This is duct tape,

sometimes known as duck tape.

It will stick to your fingers

but to nothing useful.

                      The whistle *is* useful

                      for attracting attention,

                        most of which will

                            prove unwanted.

In the thermos you may keep

hot drinks warm

and cold drinks cool,

but   the   water   will   poison
you.

          Ah, the rope, the rope, Let us leave the rope, 'til the end of hope.

                      Meals ready to eat,

                      MREs in military speak.

                      You have two packets

                      due to space limitations.

This watch has no battery

it is not self-winding:

you will have to be

awake, when it stops.

                                                  You have a torch

                                                  - and batteries.

                                          It is your source of light,

                                             at least for a week

                                              of winter nights.

Here is your first aid kit,

you will die of sepsis,

before you find anything

to close your cuts firmly.

                          The king of knives!

                  as issued to the Swiss Army

                        - neutral for centuries.

                      It has a tool to remove

                    something from the hoof

                 of the horse you have eaten.

This is a simple lighter

a zippo, filled with fuel.

While you have it,

you can burn things.

perhaps wood,

perhaps furniture,

certainly what bridges are left.

ABANDONED FLOWERS

Your final item is

the last great invention,

left to mankind.

A clockwork radio

to listen to The Buzzer

on the short wave,

long after the voices

fall silent.

There, At The World's End

There, at the world's end,

we'll stir tea with coffee spoons,

eat cress and blue-cheese sandwiches

in the fading afternoons.

We'll conduct a choir of mermaids,

in the songs we always sang,

listening for the whimper,

for we dare not risk the bang.

There'll be no Little Gidding,

and no cricket on the Green,

we'll wish for parish broadsheets

and politely vented spleen.

There, beside the final shore,

we'll curse in fluent Walloon,

and watch the last of all humanity

idly pissing on the moon.

Urban(e) Voodoo

I use Tiffany pins

and Lankton did my dolls.

My gris gris contains emeralds,

I serve only the better class of souls.

I'm as regal as

Marie was, I put my

blood in your cappucino.

Better lay a vacuum 'cross the doorway.

I keep my Jimson

in Lalique. I cut my

sister's husband's Berluti shoes.

She still lives alone with her Siamese cats.

I come expensive,

you northern fool.

There is nothing

I can't expedite.

Shoah And Tell

Down streets too clean

for challah, kreplach or sauerbraten,

a man must go lightly towards his fate.

Under the moon and lamplit rooves and spires,

while rat meets cat beside middens, pails

and mülltonnen, where then meets now,

just this side of memory,

Kurt or Bernd or even Siegried flicks a butt

– a red firefly landing in a muddy puddle.

The tocsin rings the new day in,

church-bells toll the curfew's beginning.

A crystal smash of windows

told innocents it was time

and time again

that such things happened.

People spill out of the Ratskeller;

rats scurry back to alleys,

allies of the sinister cats,

familiars to the jackbooted warlocks

casting runes in gothic script,

and spells over Lumpenvolk.

ABANDONED FLOWERS

"*Ein Volk, Ein Reich, Ein Führer,*
Ein Ei dottereich und Rührer!" *

The little Corporal wore his motley
as pied as any piper's:
we listened to the thrilling tune
leading Júden to their doom.

*"One people, one Reich, one Leader,
A double-yolked egg and a scrambler".

Friday At 8

Chit-chat-chatter crosses candle-sticked, cloth-covered table.

The bored smiles below dead-eyes roam clock-wise

towards the ticking antique in the corner of the room.

The guttering flames dispel no gloom,

tasteful recessed spots – so last year -

shine down on every wisely turned deaf-ear.

Attention wavers, attention waivers

are brandished in the form of subject change

and these same leap within a titan's range.

What was Papa driving off the road in Burgos? Say-at?

Fiat, or Hispano Suiza? Gazes turn to Tom's Louisa:

'A conjuring trick with bones!'

her suffering partner groans.

Speak not of religion, politics and love,

though this unholy trinity is joined, unwanted,

by property and equity and debt in perpetuity.

Above the candles, above his head, the inherited, increasing crown:

while over undiscovered lovers with arrangements undisclosed,

bored to omniscience, the starved look down

at other carefully chosen guests, whose case rests

in one moment's silence, before infinite jests

and "did you knows?" rush to fill the dreaded void

and the hostess looks at Tom, annoyed,

he - buoyed, by Pinot Grigot, and powdered brio -

gives account of Castel del Rio,

or was it Cannes? Dreadful man, how on earth Louisa can

stand him around or even a round at the after hours club

where both will go to scrape and rub

the nearness of others, that private hell,

of a dinner party that went so well.

Jake and Rupert strangely placed, perhaps they should be faced,

not by each others' side, an insult to their pride, Tom for instance

is far from Louise, Rupert thinks some prejudice is traced,

in putting only them together, and it is not chance,

that in some bizarre and ritual dance

they know they are not in the gang.

Hang their mores, their narrow minds,

their showing we are not quite their kind,

by not separating us. The boys will bicker on the bus,

through Notting Hill as far as Hampstead,

and all the polite talking will be wasted.

 Mine host, insubstantial as a ghost, fills glasses,

passes a hand through thinning hair,

fixes the ceiling with a stare,

sees the hostess, lower lip slack,

thank God for the percodan for her back

when we were seventeen, I love you still, Irene, Irene.

Words from long forgotten songs,

George stifles a yawn, prolongs

the moment between, memory and mentioning

the after-dinner drink, do not give them time to think,

the world is spinning, spinning, it makes you dizzy

to think about the centripetal force that must apply

though we hold on only by our fingers, by

our fingernails.

♀ ♂

Upward, ever upward,

sparks fly: the centre

will not matter.

Ring-a-ring a rosebud,

George remembers that

and what it means

with distant, darkened pleasure.

♀ ♂

The crockery cleared, the knives sheathed

all candles snuffed, and snifters quaffed,

go then gently after 'goodnight!'

And shut the door, shut the door on them

and your shared dreams

from which you woke to find yourself giving parties

for people like your parents.

These Are The End Times

One quartet is assembled,

grazing in desultory fashion.

The world turns, the world burns,

the gate is open, the horses ride,

fleshed out from their time at pasture.

Pestilence comes in silent waves,

Ebola, Cholera, Dysentery.

Famine feasts on fly-blown Africa;

Boko Haram, beaucoup haram, very kaffir.

War ensures no Damascene conversion,

Yalla ISIL, yalla ISIS, jundi kabir.

Death comes pale at a canter,

raining fire, raining gas, raining poison.

"The horror, the horror"

"Mistah Kurtz, he tell de future"

These are the end times,

take your partners

for the Totentanz.

EWAN LAWRIE

Place your bets on the Apocalypse Stakes,

back all four to win by a nose,

watch it live or watch it dead

watch the pale horse win by a head.

Will someone throw the nuclear dice?

The Cossack-fixated former spy?

The cartoon, strange-haired, trumped-up guy?

The land is laid waste,

wasted by hollow men,

hollow vessels make most noise,

hollow demagogues with the morals of boys.

Stranded boys,

landed boys

dancing around

the head of a pig.

Unclean animal,

unclean, unclean.

The muezzin's call

is the leper's bell.

We hear, we fear,

Allah hua akhbar,
wa Mohammed a russul

If we kneel on the qibla
we bare our necks
to the swift sword.

Their virgins outnumber ours
and their women quake in fear
while ours protest
- but not enough -
at mutilations
that are no more
religious
than
a pierced navel
or a prison tattoo.

B A N G!
This IS how it ends.
My whimpering friends.

Faces

Older, slower, less tolerant,

I start this poem

in a here-and-now

place and time.

I flinch at any direct gaze

returned by the ancient

in the looking glass -

baggy-eyed and grey -

he reproaches me.

Slurp! Slap! Snap! Scrap!
Beer, birds, words, herds.
Joining in is fitting in.
Joining up is giving up.

24-hour party propagandists,
improving the City of the Bear's
reputation for decadence:
I drink all night
and sometimes the next day.

ABANDONED FLOWERS

Wake up in East Anglia,
fall into bed East of Suez,
feeling I'm East of Eden,
reading lines from East Coker.

The boredom, the not-quite-fighting a war-dom,
the medals, the battlefields flown over,
the drawn-out retreats, never called defeats,
the hotels replaced by tents in deserts,
suddenly I am Omar Khayyam.

In Spain, I am someone else again,
Professor Longhair, the Scottish teacher,
walking from class to class
on the shady side of the street.

Here is my home,
it is where I am.
All the other places, fit the faces
I wore to fit in **them.**
We are our own home.

I can almost see that handsome boy
behind the hall-of-mirror-image
grotesque, staring out at me.
He winks, I don't wink back.

The Green Man

England, their England.

Let none say our,

we've sold it by the pound,

not Ezra but sterling:

a silvered note

not tied to a gold standard,

nor a royal one at half-mast

for a year and a day,

as the faerie queen's successor,

The Second, follows her Greek Puck

to the other side of the sky.

What will happen?

The Prince of Saving Whales

will ascend the Britannic throne

transformed by coronation

into a noble, valiant figure

draped in noble causes

of the colour green.

And the tattoo-ed men,

the new druids, crazed by fluids

will wrap themselves in flags

with too much blue for their liking

striking poses for the papers

in these Parler games

for Bulldog Britons

believing the sunlit uplands

made real among the wheely bins and litter.

For the Major Oak is not their rally-point,

though they see themselves in Lincoln Green

leisure wear and slave-made Adidas trainers

standing up for the common man,

never never being slaves, unless -

but this remains unsaid

outside of dark Wetherspoon corners

with beer for breakfast

and lager for lunch

and drunk for dinner.

EWAN LAWRIE

The Green Man

will take his seasons

as they come,

his tributes as his due:

he watched Romano-Britain

crumble into rubble and rapine.

"Engaland", their "Engaland!"

Let the Pict have his woad,

blue is his colour.

Green is Engaland's colour:

the colour of envy.

Here Is Movement

Amid wind-moved leaves

raucous blackbirds bicker,

tumble from a branch,

remember to stop

brawling in time

to miss the ground

and fly upwards,

orange beaks sparking

in the grey day.

In the gutter,

a reddish-squirrel lies:

it could be sleeping,

though it is not.

I spy his brother

running on a branch

and I want him

to be careful

lest he fall too.

A reusable bag,

urban tumbleweed,

rolls between the Edge

and the Rec;

chased by wrappers

discarded by the careless,

or left behind by

orange-jacketed men

of kinetic haste.

Acknowledgements

With thanks to ABCTales. A place of encouragement, experimentation and even excellence. I don't pretend to the latter, but I've had the benefit of the first and indulged in the second.

https://www.abctales.com/

Also By Ewan Lawrie

Poetry

Last Night I Met John Adcock Published by Cerasus Poetry short-listed for the Welsh Poetry Prize 2020

Novels

The Moffat Trilogy

Gibbous House

No Good Deed

At The Back Of The North Wind

https://amzn.to/3Xm97xd

Other Novels

Smokescreen

Fools Rush In

Short Stories

In The Mouth Of The Bear

Café Corto

https://amzn.to/42hSvYL

Printed in Great Britain
by Amazon